Loved As You Are
Companion Guide

Written by Steven & Courtney Cohen
Illustrated by Akshay Jugdhar

Loved As You Are - Companion Guide

Copyright © 2023 by Steven & Courtney Cohen

Written by: Steven & Courtney Cohen

Characters created by: Steven Cohen, Courtney Cohen, - Reece Cohen, Shelby Cohen, and Makayla Cohen

Illustrated by: Akshay Judghar

Layout by: Steven Cohen

Published by Now Found Publishing, LLC

Southlake, Texas

NowFoundPublishing.com

ISBN: 978-1-942362-29-6

All rights reserved. No part of this book may be reproduced or transmitted in any form or by any means, electronic or mechanical, including photocopying, and recording, or by and information storage and retrieval system, without permission in writing from the publisher.

Dear Parents, Teachers, Family, and Counselors

(and anyone else who is reading *Loved As You Are* to a child),

We have created this guide to help you and your child process in depth the poem and illustrations you will encounter in **Loved As You Are**. This book addresses real situations that your child has likely encountered. We want to equip you with questions, talking points, and a fun scavenger hunt so you and your child can get the most from **Loved As You Are**.

Visit http://lovedasyouare.com to purchase your copy and for more information on Gif.

Activities in this Guide Include:

- **Scavenger Hunt** - We have hidden some Easter eggs for you to find together. Though not necessarily eggs, we hope you have fun exploring the pages with your child for these stealthy items. You'll even discover characters from our other children's books.

- **Suggested Questions** - These are simply what they sound like — topics you can discuss while reading and looking at the illustrations together. You do not need to ask every question in one sitting. Feel free to ask other questions too. Consider these as springboards into purposeful and healing conversations. You can also use Prepare Your Heart, Background, and PCR Contemplations to guide you into deeper conversations and along your own healing and freedom journey.

- **Prepare Your Heart** - We want you to know what your child may feel. While these sections are not exhaustive, they do offer some suggestions to help you put yourself in their place and look at the world through their eyes. Think about times when you may have experienced these same thoughts and emotions so that you too can gain healing. In all situations, ask God what He says about you and your child's pain. Pour love and encouragement into your child as they express how they feel.

- **Background** - Here you'll discover the reasons we chose specific words or illustrations for each page.

- **PCR Contemplation** - This stands for Parent, Counselor, or Reader Contemplation. Although these are children's books, many older readers have also been profoundly impacted. Encounter ideas and concepts to think about in your own life and how your experience may affect your life and the life of this child.

Gif the giraffe was first introduced in **Where Your Beginning Began** wandering through the wilderness in the land of **Fambly** (Jamaican for Family). In **Loved As You Are**, you will discover new vantage points of this beautiful land.

Family comes in all shapes, sizes, and colors. Adoption through hard places, like foster care, is rarely easy and is one of the wonderful and challenging paths a family can walk to come together. Even the storms and steep mountains of life your child has faced are part of the larger, colorful portrait God is painting of their life. Though God may not have brought the challenges their way, He can always make use of them for your child's good.

Join **Gif**, the giraffe, on his perilous and providential journey to find his forever home – to discover what it means to be loved as you are.

What to Expect: Like adoption, **Loved As You Are** is a fun, colorful land which still has some perilous and challenging places as you travel throughout all our Land of Fambly books.

Our family has personally experienced the beauty and challenges of foster care and adoption, which prompted us to share this book with you and the children you love. In this guide, we'll walk you through the book, page by page, to help you see the many hidden gems that can springboard helpful and healing conversations with your child.

Grab your copy of **Loved As You Are** and join us for the scavenger hunt, deep questions, and guidance to help you in self-reflection.

Sincerely,

Steven & Courtney Cohen

If you need resources on how to handle these topics, please contact us at www.nowfound.org. We are not licensed counselors and do not claim to be able to provide psychological or clinical treatment or diagnoses. If a conversation triggers your child, please seek professional help. In case of emergency, please contact your local emergency services.

Prepare Your Heart

In this first Prepare Your Heart section, we want to prepare your heart not only for this book, but for adoption as a whole.

As parents, we need to develop a heart that encourages curiousity and deep discussion and welcomes questions of identity, culture, and heritage. We should welcome and not be afraid of questions like:

- Why do bad things happen?
- How do I deal with pain?
- Do I belong?
- How am I going to get through hard times?

We also want to honor the heritage our children carry. Their birthparents matter in ways that you may or may not understand, whether or not they're in the picture of day-to-day life. Only their unique comingling of DNA could produce this precious child. And, through these questions and considerations, we always want to point our children back to the original Source – God.

PCR Contemplation

In this first section for contemplation, like the above Prepare Your Heart, we hope you will contemplate on these questions about adoption in general and how you can help, whether that is fostering, adopting, supporting those who do, or introducing others to the beauty of family through fostering and adoption.

Often our children, like so many children of God, think that love is earned or is dependent on our performance. Our desire is not only that your children would know, but that you as well would know that you are loved in your messiness, failures, and incredible beauty – just as you are.

Gift Page:

Suggested Questions:
You may want to ask your child if they want to write their name, so they feel a deeper connection when they look back on this book as they grow.

Prepare Your Heart
The dots and spots of various shapes and sizes throughout this book represent the uniqueness of your child – not just their physical appearance, but of who they were created to be, their character, their history, their experiences, and pain. It is up to you to look past the easy to see colors and markings on your child, asking God to reveal who they really are and how they really feel.

Background
You'll note on the first page an opportunity to write to whom this book is presented, who it's from, and when. This book is intended to belong to the child as they carry it through life, reminding them of who they are, where they came from, and the people who love them.

Title Page:

Suggested Questions:
- What do you think the giraffe's name is?
    - Follow-up: The answer is Gif (pronounced Jif).
- Why do you think his name is Gif?
    - Follow-up: Because his coloring looks like peanut butter.

Prepare Your Heart
The ambiguity of life is often challenging, but sometimes permanency is even greater. Although the thought of adoption is beautiful, we also need to remember it can also be the death of a hope for reunification, restoration, healing, and a life no longer available. Often, that permanency can create a different sort of ambiguity and cause a child to question everything they know, everything they believe themselves to be, and even make them believe they need to try to be someone they are not.

Background
Below the title, you'll see Gif, the adorable and fun giraffe. Gif the giraffe, pronounced Jif, was first painted on our nursery room wall as we prepared for our first adopted daughter's arrival. He gained his name almost three years later when she would say goodnight to the animals, and she called him peanut butter. Like that creamy substance on the roof of your mouth, the name just stuck.

PCR Contemplations
Take a moment and think about how your child's experiences in life have changed. Take off your proverbial lenses and think about how they may see you, their CPS worker, the judge, or even themselves. Now ask God what He says about these people and how He can use you to bring His love into their lives. Ask how He wants to instill His desire for your child in their heart.

Scripture Page

Scavenger Hunt:
The stone is a drawing found later in the book. See if you and your child can find it along the way. (It can be found on page 9 of the poem, where Gif is dreaming about what his family will look like and draws it on the wall.)

Background:
We wanted to include Dream Rock at the beginning of the book to welcome our kids to dream, to look for God to show them His dreams and desires for their life.

1 Corinthians 13:4-8 is a life verse for me (Steven). It speaks to what love is and isn't and what it does and doesn't do. When I was a hate-filled, atheistic anti-Christ, God showed me the number 1134 multiple times a day, almost every day. Upside down that number reads hEll, but when I asked God what it meant, He had something much more powerful and important for me. He took me to this verse to tell me He loved me. No matter how horrible I acted, no matter how far I thought I was from God, no matter how unforgivable I thought my actions and thoughts were, He loved me. We include this as the vision for this book because no matter what you have gone through, no matter what your child has done, God loves you and loves them. Let them know that today, and every day, as you read this to them.

When one day you wonder,
Whether you belong,
Please know you're a part of
God's portrait beautifully drawn.

The Unfinished Portrait

Scavenger Hunt
- How many spots does Gif have?
    - Answer: 90

Suggested Questions
- Would you rather be four feet or ten feet tall? Why?
- What do you think about family?
    - Follow-up: Discuss why your child feels that way.
- What do you think Gif is thinking about?
    - Follow-up: How do you think Gif feels?
- Who is drawing this picture?
    - It's God's hand completing the portrait.
    - Follow-up: What do you think is in the swirling, unfinished area?

Prepare Your Heart
With their entire world swirling around them, our children often struggle to see the larger picture. As parents, teachers, counselors, friends, and family we have the opportunity, honor, and responsibility to help them process their surroundings.

Background
- Welcome to the land of Fambly!
    - Our youngest daughter (who is adopted) has a Jamaican heritage, which we sought to honor in this name.
- We begin the story with, "When one day you wonder," because we want to give our children permission to wonder, to dream, to ask hard questions, and most importantly to see us as a safe place where they can bring all these topics.
- Gif is looking off in the distance, wondering where he is, where he is going, and if he belongs. He sees an unformed and clouded future, struggling to see anything beyond the cliff he currently stands on.
- The hand with a paintbrush is God drawing out Gif's portrait, his story, step by step, and as we will see on the last page, creates a beautiful portrait of Gif's life.

PCR Contemplation
- Much like how we struggle from time to time, Gif is struggling with the unknown and how to reconcile the hard things he has gone through with the existence of an all-knowing, all-loving God.
- What stories can you tell that will assure your child of God's love for them?

*On God's canvas
He finds use in each hue;
Blending the light and the dark,
All is beauty from His view.*

Blending the Light and the Dark

Scavenger Hunt
- Keep your eyes out for the Lion
    ◦ Each time you see the Lion we are calling your attention to God's love for us found in John 3:16, "that God so loved the world that He gave His only son, Jesus," the Lion of Judah.
- Find all the Carrot Trees
    ◦ There are 13 of these uniquely shaped trees, only found in the land of Fambly.

Suggested Questions
- Would you rather always have daytime or nighttime? Why?
- Which do you like better, the light or dark page?
    ◦ Follow-up: What makes that better?
- What is the difference between the two?
- How do you feel about the other side?

Prepare Your Heart
Your child may not be able to see the good in what has happened, and it may even be difficult for you. However, God is with us even in the difficult times and uses every bit of our lives as part of our overall story. That shows just how much He loves us.

Background
This scene is illustrated to show that both the light and dark times in our lives are still beautiful. That may not be the case if we are looking at those events through the paradigm of the pain experienced. Much like the lava, glowing and possibly scary, extremely hot and dangerous, it is what created the beautiful landscape we see in the light.

PCR Contemplation
- As children, we often think in absolutes – in black and white – that things are either good or bad. But with maturity, we are better equipped to see the many shades and hues in between. Just because we face difficult situations doesn't mean they're entirely bad.
- God promises in Romans 8:28 that "God works all things for the good of those who love Him and are called according to His purpose." God may not be the cause of what we interpret as "bad" things in our lives, but He does allow them. If He didn't, we would be stripped of free will and incapable of true and chosen love. Despite this, free will coupled messy people often leads to hurt. In His goodness, God promises that He will take ALL things - what we interpret as "good" and "bad" - and He will make them all come out for our good in the end.
- Think back to a time in your life when circumstances felt dark, scary, or uncertain. With the benefit of hindsight, what good are you now able to see that emerged from that time?

Scavenger Hunt
- Is there anyone here with Gif?
    - Follow-up: What do you think it is?
    - Answer: An alligator
- What do Gif and the Lion have in common?
    - Answer: A heart on their tails. You may have to look at other pages to see.

Suggested Questions
- How do you think Gif is feeling right now?
- When you feel sad do you also feel alone?
- Did you know that even when we feel alone, we aren't?
    - Do you think an alligator could help Gif?
    - Follow-up: Sometimes the person we least expect can be our greatest helper or friend.

Prepare Your Heart

It's so special when our children are filled with happiness and joy, but it is also okay for our children to be sad, hurt, angry, and tired. It's also okay to experience other emotions that are harder to understand or work through. This section of the book gives you an opportunity to talk about things that make them sad without dismissing them. It's a time to allow them to give you a glimpse into their world. Be aware of your response so that you don't shut that portal. It is also a great time to let them know that they are never alone. God is always with us; and there are many instances when He provides an unexpected someone (like the alligator in this scene) to be exactly who we need.

Background

Take note of how far back you can see the giant lily pads. We wanted to create a depth to this image because people are deep. While there may be something shiny and glistening up close, it may not be what needs to be focused on right now.

PCR Contemplation

- Emotions themselves are neither good nor bad. When we feel sad, there is nothing wrong with the emotion. It is simply an indicator that something is or isn't going as expected. Emotions don't need to define us. They can simply remind us to slow down and pay attention.
- What difficult emotion do you most commonly struggle with? What do you think it may be pointing to in your life that you need help with?

Diverse Friends and Family

*If ever you wonder
Whether anyone cares,
If there's a place for you
You need only count the prayers.*

Scavenger Hunt
- How many babies can you find?
    - Answer is 8 (including the owl eggs). We believe children are children even before they are born, just like our owls do.
- Can you find markings from the mommies and daddies that show in their kiddos?
    - Notice the Panther & Leopard cub has mixed markings. If you look close enough you will see the baby elephant's ears are a mixture of its mom and dad too.

Suggested Questions
- Would you rather be around a lot of people or just a few?
    - How do you think the animals feel as they all get together?
    - Follow-up: How do you feel when you are with larger groups?
- What makes you feel happy or loved?
- What parts of you come from your birth mom & birth dad?
    - What's your favorite part about yourself?

Prepare Your Heart

As we place ourselves in our child's world, we may realize how easy it is to question if anyone really cares about them. Now that we have discussed never being alone and finding support and friends in unexpected places, let's shift to being intentional about finding those people. It is important to start thanking God for the people He has placed around us. You may also want to let your child know that you love the parts that they like about themselves and that you are so glad that your child looks like their birth parents.

Keep an eye out throughout the book to locate beautiful environments that can seem treacherous or harmful when you change the atmosphere. Notice the beauty of Fambly Peaks as the sun gleams over its hills. This may change in the upcoming illustrations.

Background

In this spread we see some of the friends and families found in Fambly. They may look different, many of them blended versions of their parents. We wanted to show more of the characters from Fambly and to show the beautiful diversity found there, much like in our world.

PCR Contemplation

- In a world of curiosity, people make insensitive comments like, "Oh is he/she adopted?" Or "Do you know who his/her real parents are?" Comments like those can support the notion that people just don't care, but in reality, people often don't know what to say. When we feel that people don't care, we need to take a closer look at those around us. They may not be perfect, but there are people who love us in beautiful ways.
- In those moments, you have an opportunity to help give people better language. For example, in our family, we have two biological and one adopted. To the stranger in the grocery store asking if my daughter who doesn't look like me is adopted, I may say, "Yes - we prayed for so long and God gave us this gift!" Or I might tease them a bit with, "What makes you ask that? We look identical." To someone who mentions her "real" parents, I might respond like this: "We are her real parents. I think you're referring to her biological parents, who are also her real parents. They had a real role in bringing her into this world and we have a real role in raising her."
- We also need to take a deep look at our children and find aspects of them and their birth parents that we can honor. Being thankful for their birth parents should not be hard to do. If nothing else, we can continue to be grateful that they chose life.

When searching for reason,
For a design to be,
Know you are an answer
To so many prayers from me.

Dreaming of Family

Scavenger Hunt
- Have you seen this rock before?
    - If you look back, it was at the beginning of the book.
- We aren't done with Dream Rock quite yet. Keep your eyes out as you continue to read but know that it may look a little different when you see this scene next time.

Suggested Questions
- Who do you think Gif is drawing on Dream Rock?
    - Answer: Gif is dreaming of having a family full of love and acceptance.
- Who do you think the two giraffes are?
    - Answer: Those are the adoptive parents dreaming about their child, Gif.
- What are they playing with?
    - Answer: They are dreaming of their future child, building him or her out of rocks as they pray for God to expand their family.
- What do you think we dreamt about doing with you?
    - Describe some of the dreams you have had and ask your child if they sound like fun or if they would like to do those things.

Prepare Your Heart

Your child has likely been dreaming about a family for as long as you have. In this illustration we wanted to show how your family was being dreamt of by all of you. You have been dreaming of and preparing for your children while your children have been doing the same. Some deeper conversations to have with your child might be if they have ever dreamt about family; what family looks like in their dreams; what sort of things they do together; where they live and go with each other; and if and where they may go on vacation or family trips.

Background

My wife and I dreamt of fostering and adopting children before we were engaged. We knew we had dreams and desires, but it wasn't until we were in the midst of fostering that we realized they have been dreaming as well. Most often those dreams are to go back to their birth family, but when they realize that isn't happening, their dreams often shift to the things that they commonly feel are most fun or that will benefit them the most.

PCR Contemplation

What do you know about your child? Perhaps even more important, what do they know about you? To build a safe space, it may be beneficial to build common ground or to share vulnerably with them both fulfilled and dashed dreams, hopes, and desires you've experienced. It's not a competition nor comparison but should be looked at as an opportunity for connection. Knowing that you have been waiting, dreaming for them may bring comfort, but be aware that it may also come across that you hoped they would be ripped from their family or experience horrible trauma, just to fulfill your desires. Depending on the situation and beliefs of your child, it could also come across as if God prefers you over them, because He is fulfilling your dreams and desires at the expense of theirs, especially if their wounds are still very fresh. Be mindful of where your child is and how your dreams of having them may come across

Mountains of Trouble

We had hoped the journey
Would have been free from pain,
Eased of turmoil or hurt,
Without the struggles or shame.

Scavenger Hunt
- Have you seen these mountains in Fambly before?
- In this image there are just a few perspective items to consider. Take notice of the sharp, jagged cliffs and edges and the dark ominous cloud.

Suggested Questions
- Would you rather snow ski or scuba dive?
- Have you ever seen a giraffe in snow?
- How do you think Gif feels?
    - Follow-up: What do you think Gif wants right now?
- Have you ever felt like you were somewhere you didn't belong?
    - Follow-up: What would have made you feel better in those moments?

Prepare Your Heart

Like a giraffe on a snow-capped mountain, many of our foster and adopted children feel like they don't belong. Whether it is ethnic, geographic, climate, or just familial differences, it's difficult to process change, especially the massive amount of change and/or trauma our kiddos have gone through. Sometimes these changes can look impossible to overcome, but time, maturity, intentional conversations, purposeful connections, and, most importantly, God's presence can conquer these so-called insurmountable obstacles.

Background

In this scene, Gif is clearly somewhere he doesn't belong. Giraffes aren't designed to live in high, mountainous, snowy areas. Everything here is cold, sharp, treacherous, and frightening. Gif is alone as he faces this perilous environment. And the lightning storm seems to stretch out ahead of him. Life brings difficult times that we must walk through. When we face them and discuss them, we are more capable of experiencing healing. Ignoring the storm doesn't make it disappear.

PCR Contemplation

We should expect that some answers may be difficult to hear. However, consider that if it is hard to hear, how much harder it must be to share or to have experienced. When we are in the cold, loud, and perilous darkness of a storm it looks and feels much different than what it may look like in a far-off valley. When in the distance, we may look at the storm's power and beauty in awe, while hoping it doesn't come our way. Storms shake things up and make people move, while at the same time supplying life-supporting sustenance. God provides for us in the storm, even when we are running for cover.

Think about what your child has gone through and may still be going through. Have empathy for them. Understand that it is hard for them, but at the same time watch for the beautiful changes it may bring. They may not want to hear about the beauty of the storm while they are running for cover, but there will be a time when they will need it, want it, and hopefully embrace it as part of their larger story.

In the Hand of Royalty

But know this, precious one,
Before you came to be
God knew and called your name
Declaring you as royalty.

Scavenger Hunt
- Where have you seen the hand lifting Gif before?
- How many "cloud" steps are there?
    - Answer: 7, which many attribute to holiness, perfection, or completeness.

Suggested Questions
- Would you rather be a rule maker or a rule follower?
- How do you feel about royalty?
- What do you think a king or queen is responsible for?
- What would you do if you were king/queen?
    - What country would you want to rule over? Why?

Prepare Your Heart

Outside of the constructs and before the existence of time, God dreamt of your child. Their Creator is also the King of all kings. As His child, He has a royal identity to pass along to them. Children adopted from hard places often struggle with identity. They've felt unwanted and cast off by the very people who are supposed to love them most. They've felt small and helpless as unknown adults make life-altering decisions for them. As adoptive parents of these precious children, we have the honor and responsibility of helping them realign their identity to what is true – who God says they are.

Background

We wanted Gif's crown and throne to be natural to Fambly, so take note that there are no refined metals involved in their construction. It's easy to imagine that the heavenly realm is somewhere up in the clouds or someplace very far away. But the heavenly realm presented here is just on the other side of the hellish storms we saw Gif struggle through on the previous page. Notice the sharp peaks poking through the clouds. Even higher than the struggles we face is God's reality.

We also represented the hand of God in a way that would better match the Middle Eastern richness we would expect the historical Jesus to have.

PCR Contemplation

- What do you see when you look at yourself? What do you think about your value and purpose?
- This book isn't just about your children but is also about you as an adopted child of God. Do you realize that you are also royal? Romans 8:15-17 says, "For you did not receive the spirit of slavery to fall back into fear, but you have received the Spirit of adoption as sons, by whom we cry, 'Abba! Father!' The Spirit himself bears witness with our spirit that we are children of God, and if children, then heirs – heirs of God and fellow heirs with Christ, provided we suffer with him in order that we may also be glorified with him." When we give our lives to Jesus, the Father adopts us as His own children, fellow heirs with Christ. God takes us out of our dark, hopeless emptiness and beautifully grafts us into His family.

My Family Tree

You're strong, fun, and smart,
So beautifully crafted;
Into our family tree
Your roots have been grafted.

Scavenger Hunt
- Can you find Gif's spots anywhere besides on Gif?
    - Answer: They have been grafted into the roots of Gif's family.

Suggested Questions
- Would you rather climb a tree or sit in its shade?
- Who do you think the giraffes are in these pictures?
    - Answer: baby Gif, teenage Gif diving, Gif's maternal grandparents and mother, and Gif's adoptive parents' wedding.
- Do you want to get married one day?
    - Where would you like to get married?
    - Who would you want to be there with you?

Prepare Your Heart

Family trees for fostered and adopted children can be a difficult and sensitive subject. Often, we don't know the people and information needed to complete them. In addition, just putting our kiddos in our tree means they don't see themselves through their birth family in your tree. And while adoption is a beautiful grafting, we must remember that grafting requires being removed, in many cases being violently cut from something else. It is okay to remember what that old thing was/is, but unless that piece is connected to a life source it will die. If you or anyone are continually pouring death over your kiddo or their birth family, that is what they will receive and they will die inside. But if you pour life, honor, respect, prayer, generosity, kindness, joy, and love over your child and their birth family they will be affirmed in their heritage and historical identity.

Background

Children adopted from hard places often have very few pictures of their birth family. Many times, those few pictures are crumpled or torn from having been shoved quickly into trash bags for yet another moving day. Through this scene, we want to honor our kids' heritage as well as their adopted lineage. Look at the roots of the drawn tree – note the spots on a few roots. These roots symbolize a grafting has taken place. Now adopted, Gif (represented by the spotted roots) has been grafted into the larger family tree of his adopted family. But pictures showing times before he came to this family are also represented. This is one way to show that blend and honor where Gif came from.

PCR Contemplation

Adoption is portrayed as such a beautiful union throughout the Bible. God has adopted the "Gentiles" (anyone other than the Jewish people) into His family through Yeshua, the Messiah, our Rescuer. In that adoption, God grafted these children into the same tree as His originally chosen people, the Jews. Have you been grafted into God's family? Do you believe in Christ as Lord and Savior? You simply need to trust that only He can save you and give Him control of your life. If you've done this, then you too have been adopted. You share something with your child in that sense. Originally, you may or may not have wanted to be adopted, just as your child may or may not have. But through that adoption, you are now part of God's beautiful family, just as your child is now part of yours.

If you or your child wants to talk more about Jesus or salvation, feel free to reach out to us at life@nowfound.org.

Our Wonderful Star

You need to change nothing
To be loved as you are.
You are our child of God,
Our bright and wonderful star.

Scavenger Hunt
- Can you find the fourth giraffe?
    - Hint: Look in the sky.
- In what other part of the story have we seen this image?
    - Answer: It's Gif's drawing on the rocks.

Suggested Questions
- What about each giraffe is different from the others?
    - Answer: the shape of their spots, ossicones (the horn-like structures on their heads), the end of their tails, facial hair, height and overall size, etc.
    - Follow-up: What are some differences between you and me?
- What's the same about each giraffe?
    - Answer: the base color of their skin, their eyes, multi-colored spots, etc.
    - Follow-up: What are similarities we share?
- What have you dreamed about regarding being in a family?
    - Follow-up: What about our family is the same or different from your dreams?

Prepare Your Heart

Children coming from hard places often think they need to change things about themselves to be loved. Many times, having been torn from their birth family, and possibly other foster homes, these kiddos have believed lies that they aren't good enough, that they aren't wanted, and that there must be something inherently wrong with who they are. They can feel desperate for stability and fearful that if they mess up, they'll be moved again. As adoptive parents of children from hard places, we need to reassure them not only with our words, but with our actions that we love them exactly as they are. Our love must not be dependent on their performance or ability to meet our expectations. Yes, we do also have a key role as parents to help them grow and mature. But that will only successfully come as they first feel secure in our love for them.

Background

Dreaming is a precious and powerful thing. You likely dreamed about the child you would one day have. God knows our dreams and wants to not only give us the desires of our heart, but also provide a way for them to come true. While He is never the cause for the brokenness that leads to the need for adoption, He is so loving to have given adoption to help redeem what has been lost and heal what has been broken. This scene portrays those dreams of family coming to reality and being blessed by God.

Take note of the bioluminescent flowers scattered throughout the foreground. These flowers shine as a contrast to the night, just as the love you and God have shines for your child in the middle of their darker times

PCR Contemplation

- What did you dream and hope for that you do not yet see in your adopted child? Our own expectations can easily set us up for failure when we haven't surrendered them to God and asked Him to help us adjust. Are you willing to trust that God knows what your dreams are and give them to Him?
- One of the most helpful tools we have to combat disappointment from missed expectations is gratitude. Get specific and begin writing down and speaking aloud what you're thankful for regarding your child. It is absolutely amazing how quickly this shifts attitudes and perspectives away from disappointment and towards thankfulness and positivity.
- What are your child's favorite things about themselves? What are their dreams for their future? Are you willing to support and champion them even if they do not match yours? How can you support who they are and their dreams for the future?

Scavenger Hunt
- Who is signing the portrait?
    - Answer: It's God! YHWH represents Yahweh, the first name God revealed to a human (as recorded in Exodus chapter 3).
- Can you find all the previous scenes from the book in this portrait?
- Can you find Omari the orca?
    - Hint: She's on the left-hand side.

Suggested Questions
- How is this picture different from the first page when we met Gif on the cliff?
- How is this picture similar to that first scene?
- If you could go anywhere in this picture, where would you want to go?
- How do you think Gif feels now that the greater picture is revealed?
    - Follow-up: How do you think she feels now about the land all around her and beyond the portrait's edges?

Prepare Your Heart

As adults, we are better equipped to use hindsight and wisdom to see patterns throughout our life and causalities between different choices and events. Imagine yourself when you were your child's age trying to foresee what you know now. It would be difficult to conceive as a child what we can understand as an adult, including how and why certain events happened. Our lives are not merely comprised of snapshots of individual events. Rather, they are beautiful tapestries that include both easy and hard times, good and bad, celebrations and mourning, joy and sorrow.

Background

Children often live in the present moment. And those that have come from hard places can face added difficulty in having hope for the future. In the first scene of this book, we expressed the reality of the unknown and the challenging feelings a child can experience. While the first scene is full of ambiguity, we wanted to complete the portrait beautifully drawn to help instill hope in your child that life is much bigger than the present moment and that even the difficult times can become important parts of the greater picture.

While here on this page, you may want to take a moment and say hello to Omari the orca. Omari is from **However Long Forever**, our book dedicated to children found in the foster care system. With no promise of security or where they will be tomorrow, **However Long Forever** assures these beautiful children that we will love them however long they are with us and forever more.

.PCR Contemplation

- How is looking back different than looking into the future?
- Since you cannot change the past, but you can affect the future, what are you willing to put aside or change to positively invest in your family's future?
- What can you do differently today that can and will positively affect the life of your child?
- How can you show your child that God is with them every day?
- How can you show your child that their current circumstances are not the end, nor are they the totality of who they will be?

Dedication

Thank you for your part in this beautiful child's life. No matter how small or large your role is in loving this child, it is vitally important to their growth, fulfillment, healing, education, and satisfaction in life. Your prayers, service, generosity, and selfless love for them is not unnoticed and we are so thankful for you.

We hope you and your child enjoy **Loved As You Are** as much as we do. We hope this book helps facilitate many fun and healing conversations with your child as you help them put hope-filled language to their life's story. We are praying for you!

For more resources, including coloring sheets and FAQs about Now Found, please visit http://nowfound.org.

NOW FOUND
PUBLISHING

Visit
family.nowfound.org
for more
Land of Fambly
books and additional resources.

www.ingramcontent.com/pod-product-compliance
Lightning Source LLC
Chambersburg PA
CBHW081800100526
44592CB00015B/2505